50 Street Food Adventures: Flavors from Around the Globe Recipes

By: Kelly Johnson

Table of Contents

- Tacos al Pastor (Mexico)
- Banh Mi (Vietnam)
- Samosas (India)
- Pad Thai (Thailand)
- Falafel (Middle East)
- Churros (Spain)
- Arepas (Venezuela/Colombia)
- Takoyaki (Japan)
- Empanadas (Argentina)
- Kati Rolls (India)
- Bao Buns (China)
- Grilled Satay (Indonesia)
- Jamaican Jerk Chicken (Jamaica)
- Shawarma (Middle East)
- Poutine (Canada)
- Bhel Puri (India)
- Poff Poff (Nigeria)
- Croquettes (Netherlands)
- Gözleme (Turkey)
- Tteokbokki (South Korea)
- Ceviche (Peru)
- Corn on the Cob with Chili (Mexico)
- Chaat (India)
- Fish and Chips (United Kingdom)
- Kebab (Turkey/Middle East)
- Tortas (Mexico)
- Koshari (Egypt)
- Frites (Belgium)
- Grilled Cheese Sandwich (USA)
- Fried Plantains (Caribbean)
- Crêpes (France)
- Ngomok (Senegal)
- Pupusas (El Salvador)
- Momo (Nepal/Tibet)
- Carne Asada Fries (USA/Mexico)

- Dim Sum (China)
- Roti John (Singapore/Malaysia)
- Chivito (Uruguay)
- Pani Puri (India)
- Tacos de Pescado (Mexico)
- Shawarma Fries (Middle East)
- Baked Pretzels (Germany)
- Bun Rieu (Vietnam)
- Falooda (India)
- Sosaties (South Africa)
- Kue Cubir (Indonesia)
- Mango Sticky Rice (Thailand)
- Souvlaki (Greece)
- Kue Cubir (Indonesia)
- Focaccia (Italy)

Tacos al Pastor

Ingredients:

- 2 lbs pork shoulder, thinly sliced
- 3 dried guajillo chiles
- 3 dried ancho chiles
- 2 chipotle chiles in adobo
- 1/2 cup pineapple juice
- 1/4 cup white vinegar
- 1/4 cup orange juice
- 1/4 cup adobo sauce (from the chipotle chiles)
- 2 cloves garlic, minced
- 1 tsp cumin
- 1 tsp oregano
- 1/2 tsp cinnamon
- Salt and pepper, to taste
- 1 small onion, finely chopped
- Fresh cilantro, chopped
- 1 small pineapple, peeled and sliced thinly
- Corn tortillas

Instructions:

1. **Prepare the marinade:** In a skillet over medium heat, toast the guajillo, ancho, and chipotle chiles until fragrant, about 2-3 minutes. Remove stems and seeds, then place the chiles in a blender with pineapple juice, vinegar, orange juice, adobo sauce, garlic, cumin, oregano, cinnamon, salt, and pepper. Blend until smooth.
2. **Marinate the pork:** Place the thinly sliced pork in a large bowl and pour the marinade over it. Toss the pork to coat evenly. Cover and refrigerate for at least 2 hours, ideally overnight for more flavor.
3. **Grill the pork:** Heat a grill or skillet over medium-high heat. Sear the marinated pork slices, in batches if necessary, until they are browned and cooked through, about 4-5 minutes per side.
4. **Prepare the tacos:** While grilling the pork, grill the pineapple slices until lightly charred. Remove and cut them into small pieces.
5. **Assemble the tacos:** Warm the corn tortillas on the grill. Layer the grilled pork, chopped grilled pineapple, onion, and cilantro on each tortilla. Serve immediately with lime wedges and your choice of salsa.

Banh Mi (Vietnam)

Ingredients:

- 1 baguette (preferably French-style)
- 1/2 lb grilled pork, sliced (or chicken/beef for variation)
- 1/4 cup mayonnaise
- 1 tbsp soy sauce
- 1 tbsp rice vinegar
- 1 small cucumber, thinly sliced
- 1 small carrot, julienned
- Fresh cilantro sprigs
- Jalapeño, thinly sliced (optional)
- Pickled daikon radish (optional)

Instructions:

1. Slice the baguette lengthwise, but not all the way through. Lightly toast it if desired.
2. Spread mayonnaise on the inside of the bread, followed by a drizzle of soy sauce and rice vinegar.
3. Layer with the grilled pork (or protein of choice), cucumber, carrot, cilantro, jalapeños, and pickled daikon radish.
4. Serve immediately for a fresh, crunchy, and flavorful sandwich!

Samosas (India)

Ingredients:

- 2 cups boiled potatoes, mashed
- 1 cup peas, boiled
- 1 onion, finely chopped
- 2 tbsp vegetable oil
- 1 tsp cumin seeds
- 1 tsp coriander powder
- 1 tsp cumin powder
- 1 tsp garam masala
- 1/2 tsp turmeric
- 1/2 tsp chili powder
- Salt to taste
- 1 tbsp lemon juice
- 12-15 samosa wrappers or spring roll wrappers
- Oil for frying

Instructions:

1. Heat oil in a pan, add cumin seeds and chopped onions. Sauté until onions are golden.
2. Add spices (coriander, cumin, garam masala, turmeric, chili powder) and cook for a minute.
3. Add the mashed potatoes and peas, mix well, and cook for another 5-7 minutes.
4. Stir in lemon juice, adjust salt, and let the mixture cool.
5. Fill samosa wrappers with the mixture, folding them into a triangular shape. Seal edges with water.
6. Fry in hot oil until golden brown and crispy. Serve with tamarind chutney.

Pad Thai (Thailand)

Ingredients:

- 8 oz rice noodles
- 2 tbsp vegetable oil
- 2 eggs, beaten
- 1/2 lb shrimp or tofu, sliced
- 1/4 cup chopped peanuts
- 2 tbsp fish sauce
- 2 tbsp tamarind paste
- 1 tbsp sugar
- 1 tbsp lime juice
- 1/2 tsp chili flakes (optional)
- 1/2 cup bean sprouts
- Fresh cilantro, chopped

Instructions:

1. Cook rice noodles according to package instructions and set aside.
2. Heat oil in a large pan, scramble the eggs, and cook shrimp or tofu until done.
3. Add noodles, fish sauce, tamarind paste, sugar, lime juice, and chili flakes. Toss everything together.
4. Garnish with chopped peanuts, bean sprouts, and fresh cilantro.
5. Serve hot with extra lime wedges.

Falafel (Middle East)

Ingredients:

- 2 cups dried chickpeas, soaked overnight
- 1 small onion, chopped
- 2 cloves garlic, minced
- 1/4 cup fresh parsley, chopped
- 1/4 cup fresh cilantro, chopped
- 1 tsp cumin
- 1 tsp coriander
- Salt and pepper to taste
- 1 tsp baking powder
- 4-6 tbsp flour (or as needed)
- Oil for frying

Instructions:

1. Drain and rinse the soaked chickpeas, then process with onion, garlic, herbs, spices, baking powder, and flour in a food processor until coarse.
2. Let the mixture sit in the fridge for an hour to firm up.
3. Form into small balls or patties.
4. Heat oil in a deep pan and fry falafel until golden brown and crispy. Serve with pita bread, tahini, and salad.

Churros (Spain)

Ingredients:

- 1 cup water
- 1 tbsp sugar
- 1/2 tsp salt
- 2 tbsp vegetable oil
- 1 cup all-purpose flour
- 2 eggs
- 1 tsp vanilla extract
- Cinnamon sugar for coating
- Oil for frying

Instructions:

1. In a saucepan, combine water, sugar, salt, and oil, and bring to a boil.
2. Stir in the flour until the dough pulls away from the sides of the pan.
3. Remove from heat and let cool slightly before beating in eggs and vanilla.
4. Heat oil for frying. Pipe dough into hot oil and fry until golden and crispy.
5. Roll churros in cinnamon sugar and serve with chocolate dipping sauce.

Arepas (Venezuela/Colombia)

Ingredients:

- 2 cups arepa flour (precooked cornmeal)
- 2 1/2 cups warm water
- 1 tsp salt
- 1 tbsp vegetable oil
- Fillings (cheese, shredded beef, chicken, avocado, etc.)

Instructions:

1. Combine the arepa flour, warm water, and salt. Mix until dough is smooth.
2. Shape the dough into patties (about 1/2 inch thick).
3. Heat oil in a pan and cook the arepas on medium heat, 5-7 minutes per side, until golden.
4. Split open the arepas and fill them with your desired fillings (cheese, meats, etc.).
5. Serve warm.

Takoyaki (Japan)

Ingredients:

- 1 1/2 cups takoyaki flour (or all-purpose flour with dashi powder)
- 1 1/2 cups water
- 1 egg
- 1/2 tsp soy sauce
- 1/2 tsp baking powder
- 1/2 cup cooked octopus, chopped
- 1/4 cup pickled ginger, chopped
- 2 tbsp green onions, chopped
- Takoyaki sauce (or Worcestershire sauce)
- Bonito flakes and seaweed flakes for topping
- Oil for greasing

Instructions:

1. Mix the flour, water, egg, soy sauce, and baking powder to form the batter.
2. Heat a takoyaki pan and brush it with oil. Pour batter into each round compartment, filling them halfway.
3. Add octopus, pickled ginger, and green onions to each compartment.
4. Pour more batter to cover and cook, turning the balls until golden brown.
5. Drizzle with takoyaki sauce, top with bonito flakes and seaweed flakes. Serve immediately.

Empanadas (Argentina)

Ingredients:

- 1 lb ground beef
- 1 onion, finely chopped
- 1/2 cup green olives, chopped
- 1/4 cup raisins (optional)
- 1 tsp cumin
- 1 tsp paprika
- Salt and pepper to taste
- Empanada dough (store-bought or homemade)
- Oil for frying

Instructions:

1. In a pan, sauté onions until soft, then add the ground beef, cumin, paprika, salt, and pepper. Cook until browned.
2. Stir in olives and raisins (if using) and let cool.
3. Place a spoonful of the filling onto each empanada disk, fold, and seal the edges with a fork.
4. Fry in hot oil until golden brown and crispy. Serve with chimichurri sauce.

Kati Rolls (India)

Ingredients:

- 2 paratha or roti flatbreads
- 1 lb chicken or lamb, cooked and shredded
- 1 onion, thinly sliced
- 1 tomato, thinly sliced
- 1 cucumber, julienned
- Fresh cilantro, chopped
- 1 tbsp chaat masala
- 1 tbsp lemon juice
- 1/4 cup yogurt or mint chutney
- Salt and pepper to taste

Instructions:

1. Heat the paratha or roti on a hot skillet until warm.
2. In a bowl, combine the shredded meat with chaat masala, lemon juice, and a pinch of salt.
3. Layer the paratha with the spiced meat, onion, tomato, cucumber, and cilantro.
4. Drizzle with yogurt or mint chutney and roll up the paratha to encase the filling.
5. Serve immediately, wrapped in paper or foil for easy eating.

Bao Buns (China)

Ingredients:

- 2 cups all-purpose flour
- 1/2 cup warm water
- 1 tbsp sugar
- 1 tsp dry yeast
- 1/4 tsp baking powder
- 1 tbsp vegetable oil
- 1/2 tsp salt
- Filling of choice (braised pork belly, vegetables, or chicken)

Instructions:

1. In a bowl, mix warm water, sugar, and yeast. Let it sit for 5 minutes until frothy.
2. Add flour, baking powder, oil, and salt to the yeast mixture. Knead into a soft dough and let rise for 1 hour.
3. Punch down the dough and divide it into small balls. Roll each ball into a flat circle.
4. Place your filling in the center of each dough circle and fold the edges over, pinching them together to form a bun.
5. Steam the buns for 10-15 minutes until cooked through. Serve with your favorite dipping sauce.

Grilled Satay (Indonesia)

Ingredients:

- 1 lb chicken, beef, or tofu, cut into cubes
- 2 tbsp soy sauce
- 1 tbsp peanut butter
- 2 cloves garlic, minced
- 1 tbsp brown sugar
- 1 tbsp lime juice
- 1 tsp turmeric
- Skewers (wooden or metal)

Instructions:

1. In a bowl, mix soy sauce, peanut butter, garlic, brown sugar, lime juice, and turmeric.
2. Add the meat or tofu cubes to the marinade and let them soak for at least 30 minutes.
3. Thread the marinated cubes onto skewers.
4. Preheat the grill and cook the skewers for 5-7 minutes per side until charred and cooked through.
5. Serve with a side of peanut sauce for dipping.

Jamaican Jerk Chicken (Jamaica)

Ingredients:

- 4 chicken thighs or breasts
- 2 tbsp allspice
- 1 tbsp thyme
- 1 tsp cinnamon
- 1/2 tsp nutmeg
- 2 cloves garlic, minced
- 1/2 tsp ginger, grated
- 1/4 cup soy sauce
- 2 tbsp brown sugar
- 1 lime, juiced
- 1-2 scotch bonnet peppers, chopped (or other hot pepper)
- Salt and pepper to taste

Instructions:

1. In a blender or food processor, combine allspice, thyme, cinnamon, nutmeg, garlic, ginger, soy sauce, brown sugar, lime juice, scotch bonnet peppers, salt, and pepper. Blend until smooth.
2. Coat the chicken in the jerk marinade and let it sit for at least 2 hours, or overnight for more flavor.
3. Grill or bake the chicken at 400°F for 25-30 minutes, turning occasionally until cooked through.
4. Serve with rice and peas or your favorite side dish.

Shawarma (Middle East)

Ingredients:

- 1 lb chicken, lamb, or beef, thinly sliced
- 2 tbsp olive oil
- 1 tbsp lemon juice
- 2 cloves garlic, minced
- 1 tbsp cumin
- 1 tbsp paprika
- 1 tsp ground coriander
- 1/2 tsp turmeric
- Salt and pepper to taste
- Pita bread or flatbreads
- Toppings: cucumber, tomato, onion, lettuce, tahini sauce

Instructions:

1. In a bowl, mix olive oil, lemon juice, garlic, cumin, paprika, coriander, turmeric, salt, and pepper.
2. Coat the meat in the marinade and let it sit for at least 30 minutes.
3. Grill or pan-fry the meat slices until crispy and cooked through.
4. Serve the shawarma in pita or flatbread with fresh vegetables and a drizzle of tahini sauce.

Poutine (Canada)

Ingredients:

- 4 cups frozen French fries
- 1 cup cheese curds
- 2 cups beef gravy (homemade or store-bought)

Instructions:

1. Cook the French fries according to package instructions or until golden and crispy.
2. Heat the beef gravy in a saucepan.
3. Once the fries are ready, place them on a serving dish and top with cheese curds.
4. Pour hot gravy over the fries and cheese curds.
5. Serve immediately while hot and enjoy the perfect Canadian comfort food!

Bhel Puri (India)

Ingredients:

- 2 cups puffed rice
- 1/2 cup sev (crispy chickpea noodles)
- 1/4 cup boiled potatoes, chopped
- 1/4 cup onions, finely chopped
- 1/4 cup tomatoes, chopped
- 1/4 cup cucumber, chopped
- 1-2 tbsp tamarind chutney
- 1 tbsp coriander chutney
- Salt and chaat masala to taste
- Fresh cilantro for garnish

Instructions:

1. In a large bowl, combine puffed rice, sev, potatoes, onions, tomatoes, and cucumber.
2. Add tamarind chutney and coriander chutney, and mix well.
3. Season with salt and chaat masala to taste.
4. Garnish with fresh cilantro and serve immediately for a crispy, tangy snack!

Poff Poff (Nigeria)

Ingredients:

- 2 cups all-purpose flour
- 1/2 cup sugar
- 1 tsp yeast
- 1/4 tsp nutmeg
- 1/4 tsp cinnamon
- 1/2 cup warm water
- 1/2 tsp salt
- Oil for frying

Instructions:

1. In a bowl, combine flour, sugar, yeast, nutmeg, cinnamon, and salt.
2. Gradually add warm water and mix to form a smooth batter. Let it sit for 1-2 hours until it rises.
3. Heat oil in a deep pan. Scoop small amounts of batter into the hot oil, shaping them into round balls.
4. Fry until golden brown, then drain on paper towels.
5. Serve warm as a sweet, crispy treat.

Croquettes (Netherlands)

Ingredients:

- 2 cups mashed potatoes (cooled)
- 1 cup cooked chicken, minced (or beef, ham, or cheese)
- 1/4 cup parsley, chopped
- 1/2 tsp nutmeg
- Salt and pepper to taste
- 1 egg, beaten
- 1 cup breadcrumbs
- Oil for frying

Instructions:

1. Mix mashed potatoes, minced chicken (or other filling), parsley, nutmeg, salt, and pepper.
2. Shape the mixture into small cylinders or balls.
3. Dip the croquettes in beaten egg and coat with breadcrumbs.
4. Heat oil in a pan and fry the croquettes until golden and crispy, about 3-4 minutes.
5. Serve with mustard or your favorite dipping sauce.

Gözleme (Turkey)

Ingredients:

- 2 cups all-purpose flour
- 1/2 tsp salt
- 3/4 cup warm water
- 2 tbsp olive oil
- 1 cup spinach, chopped
- 1/2 cup feta cheese, crumbled
- 1/2 cup ground lamb or beef (optional)
- 1 onion, finely chopped
- Salt and pepper to taste
- Olive oil for cooking

Instructions:

1. In a bowl, mix flour, salt, warm water, and olive oil to form a dough. Knead until smooth and let it rest for 30 minutes.
2. While the dough rests, sauté the onion and meat (if using) in olive oil until cooked. Add spinach and cook until wilted, then remove from heat and stir in feta cheese. Season with salt and pepper.
3. Roll the dough into small balls and flatten each ball into a thin circle.
4. Place a spoonful of the filling on one half of the dough, fold it over, and seal the edges.
5. Heat a little olive oil in a skillet and cook the gözleme on both sides until golden brown and crispy.
6. Serve hot with yogurt or a side salad.

Tteokbokki (South Korea)

Ingredients:

- 1 lb chewy rice cakes (tteok)
- 1 tbsp vegetable oil
- 1/2 onion, sliced
- 1/2 cup fish cakes, sliced (optional)
- 2 tbsp gochujang (Korean chili paste)
- 1 tbsp soy sauce
- 1 tbsp sugar
- 2 cups water or dashi stock
- 1 tsp sesame oil
- Sesame seeds for garnish
- Chopped green onions for garnish

Instructions:

1. Soak the rice cakes in warm water for 30 minutes if they are hard.
2. In a large pan, heat the vegetable oil over medium heat. Add the onion and sauté until soft.
3. Add the fish cakes (if using) and cook for a few more minutes.
4. Stir in gochujang, soy sauce, sugar, and water or dashi stock. Bring the sauce to a boil.
5. Add the soaked rice cakes and simmer for 10-15 minutes, until the sauce thickens and the rice cakes are soft.
6. Drizzle sesame oil over the dish and garnish with sesame seeds and chopped green onions before serving.

Ceviche (Peru)

Ingredients:

- 1 lb fresh white fish (such as snapper or bass), diced
- 1/2 cup freshly squeezed lime juice
- 1/4 cup lemon juice
- 1/2 red onion, thinly sliced
- 1-2 fresh chilies (such as jalapeño or serrano), minced
- 1/2 cup fresh cilantro, chopped
- 1/2 cup corn kernels (optional)
- Salt and pepper to taste

Instructions:

1. In a bowl, combine the fish with lime juice and lemon juice. Ensure the fish is fully submerged. Let it marinate in the fridge for 30-60 minutes, until the fish turns opaque.
2. Add the red onion, chilies, and cilantro to the fish. Mix gently.
3. Season with salt and pepper, then add corn if desired.
4. Serve the ceviche chilled, either as a starter or with tostadas.

Corn on the Cob with Chili (Mexico)

Ingredients:

- 4 ears of corn, husked
- 2 tbsp butter
- 1 tsp chili powder
- 1/2 tsp cayenne pepper (optional)
- 1 tbsp lime juice
- 1/4 cup cotija cheese, crumbled
- Salt to taste

Instructions:

1. Boil the corn in salted water for 10-12 minutes until tender.
2. While the corn cooks, melt butter in a small bowl. Stir in chili powder, cayenne pepper, and lime juice.
3. Once the corn is cooked, brush each ear with the spiced butter mixture.
4. Sprinkle with cotija cheese and season with a pinch of salt.
5. Serve with extra lime wedges on the side.

Chaat (India)

Ingredients:

- 1 cup boiled potatoes, cubed
- 1 cup puffed rice
- 1/4 cup sev (crispy chickpea noodles)
- 1/2 cup chickpeas, cooked
- 1/2 cup yogurt
- 2 tbsp tamarind chutney
- 1 tbsp coriander chutney
- 1 tsp chaat masala
- 1/2 tsp cumin powder
- Salt to taste
- Fresh cilantro, chopped
- Pomegranate seeds for garnish

Instructions:

1. In a bowl, mix the boiled potatoes, puffed rice, sev, and chickpeas.
2. Drizzle the tamarind and coriander chutneys over the mixture.
3. Pour the yogurt on top and sprinkle with chaat masala, cumin powder, and salt.
4. Garnish with fresh cilantro and pomegranate seeds.
5. Serve immediately for a tangy, crunchy snack.

Fish and Chips (United Kingdom)

Ingredients:

- 4 white fish fillets (such as cod or haddock)
- 1 cup all-purpose flour
- 1/2 tsp baking powder
- 1 tsp salt
- 1/4 tsp black pepper
- 1 egg, beaten
- 1 cup cold sparkling water
- 4 large potatoes, peeled and cut into thick fries
- Oil for frying
- Malt vinegar, for serving

Instructions:

1. Heat oil in a deep fryer or large pot to 375°F (190°C).
2. For the fries, fry the potato pieces in batches for about 4-5 minutes until golden and crispy. Set aside on paper towels to drain.
3. To make the batter, mix flour, baking powder, salt, and pepper in a bowl. Add the egg and cold sparkling water, whisking until smooth.
4. Dip the fish fillets into the batter and fry them in hot oil for about 5-7 minutes, until golden brown and cooked through.
5. Serve the fish and chips with malt vinegar for drizzling.

Kebab (Turkey/Middle East)

Ingredients:

- 1 lb ground lamb or beef
- 1 onion, finely grated
- 2 cloves garlic, minced
- 1 tbsp cumin
- 1 tbsp paprika
- 1 tsp ground coriander
- Salt and pepper to taste
- Fresh parsley, chopped
- Skewers (wooden or metal)

Instructions:

1. In a bowl, combine the ground meat, grated onion, garlic, cumin, paprika, coriander, salt, pepper, and parsley.
2. Mix well and form the mixture into kebab shapes, either on skewers or as patties.
3. Grill the kebabs over medium-high heat for about 5-7 minutes per side, until cooked through and browned.
4. Serve with pita, yogurt, or a salad.

Tortas (Mexico)

Ingredients:

- 4 bolillo rolls (or soft baguettes)
- 1 lb cooked and shredded pork, beef, or chicken
- 1/2 avocado, sliced
- 1/2 onion, thinly sliced
- 1 tomato, sliced
- 1/4 cup refried beans
- 2 tbsp mayonnaise
- 1-2 tbsp salsa (optional)
- Jalapeños (optional)

Instructions:

1. Slice the bolillo rolls lengthwise, leaving one side hinged.
2. Spread mayonnaise on one half of the bread and refried beans on the other.
3. Layer the meat, avocado, onion, tomato, and jalapeños (if using).
4. Add salsa to taste, then press the sandwich together and grill it on a hot skillet for 2-3 minutes per side, until the bread is crispy.
5. Serve with extra salsa and pickled vegetables on the side.

Koshari (Egypt)

Ingredients:

- 1 cup rice
- 1/2 cup lentils (green or brown)
- 1 cup elbow macaroni
- 1 onion, thinly sliced
- 2 tbsp vegetable oil
- 1 can (14 oz) crushed tomatoes
- 2 garlic cloves, minced
- 1 tsp cumin
- 1/2 tsp coriander
- 1/2 tsp cinnamon
- 1/2 tsp allspice
- Salt and pepper to taste
- 2 tbsp white vinegar
- 2 tbsp fresh parsley, chopped

Instructions:

1. Cook the lentils in a pot of water for about 20 minutes, until tender. Drain and set aside.
2. Cook the rice according to package instructions and set aside.
3. Boil the macaroni according to package instructions and set aside.
4. In a pan, heat the vegetable oil and sauté the onion until golden and crispy. Remove the onion from the pan and set aside.
5. In the same pan, sauté the garlic, cumin, coriander, cinnamon, and allspice until fragrant. Add the crushed tomatoes and vinegar, and simmer for 10-15 minutes.
6. To assemble the koshari, layer rice, lentils, macaroni, and tomato sauce in a large serving dish. Top with the crispy onions and fresh parsley.
7. Serve hot as a main dish or side.

Frites (Belgium)

Ingredients:

- 4 large russet potatoes
- Oil for frying (vegetable or canola)
- Salt to taste
- Mayonnaise (for dipping)

Instructions:

1. Peel and cut the potatoes into thick strips.
2. Rinse the potato strips in cold water to remove excess starch, then pat them dry with a towel.
3. Heat oil in a deep fryer or large pot to 350°F (175°C).
4. Fry the potatoes in batches for about 4-5 minutes, until soft but not fully browned. Remove and drain on paper towels.
5. Increase the oil temperature to 375°F (190°C) and fry the potatoes again for another 2-3 minutes, until golden and crispy.
6. Sprinkle with salt and serve with mayonnaise for dipping.

Grilled Cheese Sandwich (USA)

Ingredients:

- 4 slices of bread (white, sourdough, or your choice)
- 2 tbsp butter
- 4 slices of cheddar cheese (or your preferred cheese)
- 1 tbsp mayonnaise (optional, for extra crispiness)

Instructions:

1. Heat a skillet over medium heat.
2. Butter one side of each slice of bread. If using mayonnaise, spread it on the other side of the bread slices.
3. Place one slice of cheese between two slices of bread, buttered sides facing out.
4. Grill the sandwich on both sides for 2-4 minutes each, until golden brown and the cheese is melted.
5. Slice and serve hot.

Fried Plantains (Caribbean)

Ingredients:

- 2 ripe plantains
- Vegetable oil for frying
- Salt to taste

Instructions:

1. Peel the plantains and cut them into diagonal slices about 1/2 inch thick.
2. Heat oil in a frying pan over medium heat.
3. Fry the plantain slices for 2-3 minutes per side, until golden brown.
4. Remove the plantains from the oil and drain on paper towels.
5. Sprinkle with salt and serve as a snack or side dish.

Crêpes (France)

Ingredients:

- 1 cup all-purpose flour
- 1 1/2 cups milk
- 2 eggs
- 1/4 tsp salt
- 1 tbsp sugar
- 2 tbsp melted butter
- Butter for cooking
- Optional fillings: Nutella, fruits, whipped cream, or jam

Instructions:

1. In a bowl, whisk together the flour, milk, eggs, salt, sugar, and melted butter until smooth.
2. Heat a non-stick skillet over medium-high heat and add a small amount of butter.
3. Pour a small amount of batter into the skillet, swirling to coat the bottom in a thin layer.
4. Cook for about 1-2 minutes until the edges begin to lift, then flip and cook the other side for 1-2 minutes more.
5. Remove from the skillet and continue with the rest of the batter.
6. Serve the crêpes with your choice of sweet fillings.

Ngomok (Senegal)

Ingredients:

- 2 cups cooked rice
- 1/2 cup ground peanuts (or peanut butter)
- 1/4 cup palm oil
- 1 onion, chopped
- 2 tomatoes, chopped
- 1 bell pepper, chopped
- 2 garlic cloves, minced
- 1 tsp ground ginger
- 1 tsp ground cumin
- Salt to taste
- 2 cups water
- Fresh cilantro for garnish

Instructions:

1. In a pot, heat the palm oil and sauté the onion, garlic, bell pepper, and tomatoes until soft.
2. Add the ground peanuts (or peanut butter) to the pot along with the ginger, cumin, and salt. Stir well to combine.
3. Add the cooked rice to the mixture, followed by water. Simmer for 10-15 minutes, stirring occasionally, until the rice has absorbed the flavors.
4. Garnish with fresh cilantro and serve.

Pupusas (El Salvador)

Ingredients:

- 2 cups masa harina (corn flour)
- 1 1/2 cups warm water
- 1 tsp salt
- 1/2 cup refried beans
- 1/2 cup cheese (mozzarella or cheese of choice)
- 1/4 cup cooked pork or chicken (optional)

Instructions:

1. In a bowl, combine the masa harina, water, and salt to form a dough.
2. Take a small portion of dough and flatten it into a disc.
3. Place a spoonful of refried beans, cheese, and optional cooked meat in the center.
4. Fold the dough over the filling and seal it, then flatten again gently into a patty.
5. Cook the pupusas on a hot griddle or skillet for about 3-4 minutes per side, until golden and crispy.
6. Serve with curtido (pickled cabbage) and salsa.

Momo (Nepal/Tibet)

Ingredients:

- 1 lb ground chicken or pork
- 1/2 onion, finely chopped
- 2 garlic cloves, minced
- 1 tsp ginger, minced
- 1/4 cup cilantro, chopped
- 1 tbsp soy sauce
- 1 tbsp sesame oil
- 1/2 tsp cumin powder
- 1/2 tsp turmeric powder
- Dumpling wrappers (store-bought or homemade)
- Salt to taste
- Steamer or pot with a steaming rack

Instructions:

1. In a bowl, mix the ground meat, onion, garlic, ginger, cilantro, soy sauce, sesame oil, cumin, turmeric, and salt.
2. Take a dumpling wrapper and place a small spoonful of the filling in the center.
3. Fold the edges over the filling and pinch them to seal the momo.
4. Steam the momos for 10-15 minutes, until cooked through.
5. Serve hot with dipping sauce (such as a spicy tomato or sesame sauce).

Carne Asada Fries (USA/Mexico)

Ingredients:

- 4 large russet potatoes, cut into fries
- 1 lb carne asada (beef flank or skirt steak)
- 1 tbsp olive oil
- 1 tsp cumin
- 1 tsp chili powder
- 1/2 tsp garlic powder
- 1/2 tsp paprika
- Salt and pepper to taste
- 1 cup shredded cheese (cheddar or Mexican blend)
- 1/2 cup guacamole
- 1/2 cup sour cream
- Fresh cilantro, chopped

Instructions:

1. Preheat the oven to 425°F (220°C). Bake the fries according to package instructions or until crispy and golden.
2. While the fries bake, heat olive oil in a skillet over medium-high heat. Season the carne asada with cumin, chili powder, garlic powder, paprika, salt, and pepper. Grill or sear the steak for 3-4 minutes per side, until medium-rare or your preferred doneness.
3. Let the steak rest for a few minutes, then slice it thinly against the grain.
4. Once the fries are done, layer them on a serving dish and top with carne asada, cheese, guacamole, sour cream, and fresh cilantro.
5. Serve immediately.

Dim Sum (China)

Ingredients:

- 2 cups all-purpose flour
- 1/2 tsp salt
- 1/4 cup hot water
- 1/4 cup cold water
- 1 tbsp vegetable oil
- 1/2 lb ground pork or shrimp
- 2 tbsp mushrooms, chopped
- 2 tbsp bamboo shoots, finely chopped
- 2 tbsp ginger, minced
- 2 tbsp soy sauce
- 1 tbsp oyster sauce
- 1 tbsp sesame oil
- 1 tsp sugar
- 1/4 tsp white pepper

Instructions:

1. In a bowl, mix the flour, salt, hot water, cold water, and oil to form a dough. Knead until smooth, then cover and let rest for 30 minutes.
2. For the filling, combine the ground pork or shrimp, mushrooms, bamboo shoots, ginger, soy sauce, oyster sauce, sesame oil, sugar, and white pepper.
3. Roll the dough into small balls and flatten into round discs.
4. Place a spoonful of filling in the center and fold the edges to seal, forming a dumpling shape.
5. Steam the dim sum in a bamboo steamer for 10-12 minutes, until cooked through.
6. Serve with soy sauce or dipping sauce.

Roti John (Singapore/Malaysia)

Ingredients:

- 2 large baguettes or crusty rolls
- 1 lb ground beef or chicken
- 1 onion, finely chopped
- 2 cloves garlic, minced
- 2 eggs
- 2 tbsp soy sauce
- 1 tbsp ketchup
- 1 tbsp mayonnaise
- 1/2 tsp black pepper
- 1/4 tsp chili powder (optional)
- Fresh cilantro for garnish

Instructions:

1. Heat a pan over medium heat and sauté the onion and garlic until softened.
2. Add the ground meat to the pan and cook until browned. Season with soy sauce, ketchup, mayonnaise, black pepper, and chili powder.
3. Beat the eggs and pour them into the pan, stirring to incorporate into the meat mixture. Cook until the eggs are fully scrambled and the mixture is cooked through.
4. Slice the baguettes into sandwich-sized pieces and lightly toast them.
5. Fill the bread with the cooked meat and egg mixture, then garnish with fresh cilantro.
6. Serve with a side of chili sauce or ketchup.

Chivito (Uruguay)

Ingredients:

- 1 lb beef steak (sirloin or flank steak)
- 4 soft sandwich rolls
- 4 slices of ham
- 4 slices of cheese (Swiss or mozzarella)
- 1 tomato, sliced
- 1/2 onion, sliced
- Lettuce leaves
- 2 tbsp mayonnaise
- 1 tbsp mustard
- Salt and pepper to taste
- Olive oil for grilling

Instructions:

1. Season the beef steaks with salt and pepper. Grill or pan-sear the steaks to your desired doneness, then set aside to rest.
2. While the steaks are resting, grill the sandwich rolls lightly.
3. Layer each roll with mayonnaise, mustard, a slice of ham, a slice of cheese, grilled steak, tomato, onion, and lettuce.
4. Close the sandwich and serve immediately.

Pani Puri (India)

Ingredients:

- 1 cup semolina (sooji)
- 1/4 cup all-purpose flour
- 1/2 tsp baking soda
- Water as needed
- 1/2 cup tamarind chutney
- 1/2 cup chickpeas, cooked
- 1/2 cup potatoes, boiled and mashed
- 1/2 tsp cumin powder
- 1/4 tsp red chili powder
- Salt to taste
- Fresh cilantro for garnish

Instructions:

1. To make the puris, mix semolina, flour, and baking soda with water to form a dough. Divide the dough into small portions and roll them into tiny balls. Flatten each ball into a small disc and fry in hot oil until crisp and golden.
2. For the filling, mix the boiled potatoes, chickpeas, cumin powder, red chili powder, and salt.
3. Carefully poke a hole in the center of each puri, then stuff with the potato and chickpea mixture.
4. Serve the pani puri with tamarind chutney and garnish with fresh cilantro.

Tacos de Pescado (Mexico)

Ingredients:

- 1 lb white fish fillets (like tilapia or cod)
- 1 cup flour
- 1 tsp paprika
- 1/2 tsp garlic powder
- 1/2 tsp cumin
- 1/2 tsp chili powder
- Salt and pepper to taste
- Corn tortillas
- Cabbage slaw (shredded cabbage, lime juice, cilantro)
- Salsa (optional)
- Lime wedges for garnish

Instructions:

1. Season the fish fillets with salt, pepper, paprika, garlic powder, cumin, and chili powder.
2. Dredge the fish fillets in flour.
3. Heat oil in a pan over medium heat and fry the fish for 3-4 minutes on each side, until golden brown and crispy.
4. Warm the corn tortillas and assemble the tacos by placing the fried fish on each tortilla, topping with cabbage slaw and salsa, if desired.
5. Serve with lime wedges.

Shawarma Fries (Middle East)

Ingredients:

- 4 large russet potatoes, cut into fries
- 1 lb chicken thighs, boneless and skinless
- 2 tbsp shawarma seasoning
- 2 tbsp olive oil
- 1/2 cup tahini
- 2 tbsp lemon juice
- 1 garlic clove, minced
- Salt and pepper to taste
- Fresh parsley for garnish

Instructions:

1. Preheat the oven to 425°F (220°C) and bake the fries until crispy.
2. Season the chicken thighs with shawarma seasoning, salt, and pepper. Cook them on a grill or in a pan with olive oil until browned and cooked through. Slice the chicken thinly.
3. Mix the tahini, lemon juice, minced garlic, and a pinch of salt to make the sauce.
4. Once the fries are ready, top them with the sliced shawarma chicken and drizzle with tahini sauce. Garnish with fresh parsley.
5. Serve immediately.

Baked Pretzels (Germany)

Ingredients:

- 1 1/2 cups warm water
- 2 1/4 tsp active dry yeast
- 1 tbsp sugar
- 4 cups all-purpose flour
- 1 tsp salt
- 1 tbsp vegetable oil
- 10 cups water
- 2 tbsp baking soda
- 1 egg, beaten
- Coarse salt for sprinkling

Instructions:

1. In a bowl, combine the warm water, yeast, and sugar. Let it sit for 5 minutes until foamy.
2. Mix in the flour, salt, and oil to form a dough. Knead the dough for about 5-7 minutes, then cover and let rise for 1 hour.
3. Preheat the oven to 450°F (230°C). In a large pot, bring 10 cups of water and baking soda to a boil.
4. Divide the dough into small pieces and roll each into a rope, then twist into a pretzel shape.
5. Boil each pretzel in the baking soda water for 30 seconds, then place on a baking sheet.
6. Brush with the beaten egg and sprinkle with coarse salt.
7. Bake for 12-15 minutes, until golden brown. Serve warm.

Bun Rieu (Vietnam)

Ingredients:

- 1 lb crab meat (or ground pork)
- 2 tbsp fish sauce
- 1/2 tsp sugar
- 2 tbsp tomato paste
- 1/2 cup vermicelli rice noodles
- 1/2 cup tofu, sliced into cubes
- 1/2 cup bean sprouts
- Fresh herbs (cilantro, mint)
- 1 lime, cut into wedges
- 4 cups chicken or pork broth
- 2 cloves garlic, minced
- 1/2 onion, chopped
- 1 tbsp vegetable oil
- Salt and pepper to taste

Instructions:

1. In a pot, heat vegetable oil over medium heat. Add minced garlic and onion, sauté until softened.
2. Add the crab meat (or ground pork) to the pot, cooking until browned.
3. Stir in the fish sauce, sugar, and tomato paste, then add the broth. Bring to a simmer.
4. In a separate pot, cook the vermicelli noodles according to package instructions, then drain and set aside.
5. To assemble, divide the noodles into bowls. Pour the broth and crab mixture over the noodles.
6. Top with tofu, bean sprouts, fresh herbs, and a squeeze of lime.
7. Serve hot and enjoy.

Falooda (India)

Ingredients:

- 2 tbsp basil seeds (sabja seeds)
- 1 cup milk
- 1 tbsp rose syrup
- 1 tbsp sweetened condensed milk
- 1/2 cup cooked vermicelli or falooda sev
- 1/2 cup ice cream (optional)
- Chopped pistachios or almonds for garnish
- Crushed ice

Instructions:

1. Soak the basil seeds in water for about 10-15 minutes until they swell up.
2. Boil the milk in a saucepan, then let it cool to room temperature.
3. In serving glasses, layer the falooda sev, soaked basil seeds, and rose syrup.
4. Pour the cooled milk and condensed milk over the layers.
5. Add a scoop of ice cream on top, then garnish with chopped pistachios or almonds.
6. Serve with crushed ice for a refreshing treat.

Sosaties (South Africa)

Ingredients:

- 1 lb chicken thighs, cut into cubes
- 1 onion, chopped
- 1 red bell pepper, chopped
- 1 green bell pepper, chopped
- 2 tbsp vegetable oil
- 1 tbsp curry powder
- 1 tbsp garam masala
- 1 tbsp paprika
- 1/2 tsp ground turmeric
- 1 tbsp lemon juice
- Salt and pepper to taste
- Skewers (wooden or metal)

Instructions:

1. In a bowl, mix together the vegetable oil, curry powder, garam masala, paprika, turmeric, lemon juice, salt, and pepper.
2. Add the chicken cubes and marinate for at least 30 minutes to an hour.
3. Thread the marinated chicken, onions, and bell peppers onto skewers.
4. Heat a grill or grill pan over medium-high heat. Grill the skewers for 10-12 minutes, turning occasionally, until the chicken is cooked through and slightly charred.
5. Serve hot with rice or bread.

Kue Cubir (Indonesia)

Ingredients:

- 1 cup all-purpose flour
- 1/2 cup rice flour
- 1/2 cup sugar
- 1/2 cup coconut milk
- 1/2 tsp pandan extract (or food coloring for a green color)
- 1/2 tsp baking powder
- A pinch of salt
- 1/4 cup shredded coconut (for topping)

Instructions:

1. In a bowl, whisk together the all-purpose flour, rice flour, sugar, baking powder, and salt.
2. Add the coconut milk and pandan extract (or food coloring) to the dry ingredients. Mix until smooth.
3. Pour the batter into greased molds or cupcake tins, filling each about halfway.
4. Steam the cakes over medium heat for about 10-15 minutes, or until a toothpick comes out clean.
5. Once cooled, top with shredded coconut before serving.

Mango Sticky Rice (Thailand)

Ingredients:

- 2 cups sticky rice (glutinous rice)
- 1 1/2 cups coconut milk
- 1/2 cup sugar
- 1/4 tsp salt
- 2 ripe mangoes, peeled and sliced
- Sesame seeds or mung beans for garnish (optional)

Instructions:

1. Rinse the sticky rice thoroughly, then soak it in water for about 1 hour.
2. Steam the rice in a bamboo or metal steamer for about 20-30 minutes, until fully cooked.
3. In a saucepan, heat the coconut milk, sugar, and salt over low heat until the sugar dissolves.
4. Pour the coconut milk mixture over the cooked sticky rice and let it absorb the liquid for about 10 minutes.
5. Serve the sticky rice with sliced mangoes on top and garnish with sesame seeds or mung beans if desired.

Souvlaki (Greece)

Ingredients:

- 1 lb pork, chicken, or lamb, cut into cubes
- 3 tbsp olive oil
- 2 tbsp lemon juice
- 1 tsp dried oregano
- 2 cloves garlic, minced
- Salt and pepper to taste
- Wooden skewers (soaked in water for 30 minutes)

Instructions:

1. In a bowl, mix olive oil, lemon juice, oregano, garlic, salt, and pepper to make the marinade.
2. Add the meat cubes to the marinade and let them marinate for at least 30 minutes.
3. Thread the marinated meat onto the skewers.
4. Grill the souvlaki skewers over medium-high heat for 8-10 minutes, turning occasionally, until the meat is cooked through.
5. Serve with pita bread, tzatziki sauce, and a side salad.

Kue Cubir (Indonesia)

Ingredients:

- 250g rice flour
- 150g sugar
- 1/2 tsp salt
- 400ml coconut milk
- 100g grated coconut (for sprinkling)
- 2-3 drops pandan extract (optional for color)
- Water (as needed)

Instructions:

1. In a mixing bowl, combine the rice flour, sugar, and salt.
2. Slowly pour in the coconut milk and stir until the mixture forms a smooth batter.
3. If you want a green color, add the pandan extract and mix well.
4. Grease a shallow baking tray and pour the batter in, smoothing it evenly.
5. Steam the mixture over boiling water for about 30 minutes, or until firm and set.
6. Once the Kue Cubir is cooked, remove it from the steamer and let it cool to room temperature.
7. Cut the Kue Cubir into small squares or rectangles, and then sprinkle with grated coconut on top before serving.

Focaccia (Italy)

Ingredients:

- 500g all-purpose flour
- 7g active dry yeast
- 1 tsp sugar
- 300ml warm water
- 50ml olive oil (plus extra for drizzling)
- 2 tsp salt
- 1 tsp dried rosemary (or fresh if preferred)
- Coarse sea salt (for sprinkling)

Instructions:

1. In a bowl, dissolve the sugar and yeast in warm water and let it sit for 5-10 minutes until frothy.
2. In a large mixing bowl, combine the flour and salt. Gradually add the yeast mixture and 2 tablespoons of olive oil, and stir until a dough forms.
3. Knead the dough on a floured surface for about 10 minutes, until it is smooth and elastic.
4. Place the dough in a greased bowl, cover it with a damp cloth, and let it rise for about 1 hour or until doubled in size.
5. Preheat the oven to 200°C (390°F). Grease a baking sheet with olive oil and stretch the dough to fit the sheet, pressing it out with your fingers to create dimples.
6. Drizzle the dough with more olive oil, sprinkle with rosemary, and season with coarse sea salt.
7. Bake for 20-25 minutes or until golden and crispy on the edges.
8. Remove from the oven and let cool for a few minutes before slicing and serving.

www.ingramcontent.com/pod-product-compliance
Lightning Source LLC
LaVergne TN
LVHW081504060526
838201LV00056BA/2923